YES, YOU CAN

Palmetto Publishing Group
Charleston, SC

Yes, You Can
Copyright © 2019 by Jamie Venturo
All rights reserved

First Edition

Printed in the United States

ISBN-13: 978-1-64111-294-9
ISBN-10: 1-64111-294-8

YES, YOU CAN

by Jamie Venturo

Illustrations by
Danielle Gruttadaurio

To Samantha, Sean and Chase,

This book is dedicated to you. Always remember
Yes, You Can!
Follow your heart and dream big!
I love you,
Mom

There once was a little girl who
wanted to try karate.
Her mother told her no!

2

Her mother said, "Try dance."
The little girl did not like dance.

5

The little girl then played soccer and
she liked it a lot. She tried softball,
track and basketball too.
She really liked all of these other sports,
but she was never the best player.

That never bothered her, she
just loved playing.

As the girl became a young lady and graduated high school, she looked for another activity or sport to try.

Every day she passed by a boxing gym. She really wanted to try boxing, but was nervous she would not fit in. There were a lot of men in the boxing gym.

11

One day she worked up the courage
to walk in and try boxing.
That was a scary thing to do.

The young lady not only loved
boxing, she was really good at it!

So, good in fact, she became both a pioneer and a champion! She was awarded Golden Gloves in New York City three times for her wins at that legendary tournament, The New York Daily News Golden Gloves. She went on to win at the national level, and then won an international tournament in Finland!

The young lady grew into a woman. That woman is me! I am married and I have three children. I wrote this book for them, and for all kids, to encourage them to try new things. If they are ever unsure if they can, I want them to think of my story, and say to themselves, "YES, I CAN!!!"

14

Are you already thinking about things you would like to try? Well, then, GO FOR IT! Work hard, have fun, and remember, "YES, YOU CAN!!!!"

ABOUT JAMIE

Jamie Venturo is the owner of Southpaw Boxing www.Southpawboxing.net and Live Free Organic www.livefreeorganic.net in Charlotte, North Carolina. Highlights of her boxing career include winning The New York Daily News Golden Gloves in 1998, 1999, and 2000; winning the U.S. Nationals, National Golden Gloves, Blue and Gold Tournament, Empire State Games and many more. Jamie was part of the first ever US Woman's National Team, where she took gold in Finland, stopping all three opponents in the first round! Jamie is married to John Venturo and has three very active children, Samantha, Sean and Chase.

Autumn
Raine

ABOUT DANIELLE

Danielle Gruttadaurio is a Forensic Artist for the Suffolk County Police Department in Long Island, New York. She is also a muralist, body painter, and an art teacher. Danielle enjoys mountain biking, running and lifting weights. She is married to Jason and has two children, Anthony Jason (AJ) and Autumn Raine.

CPSIA information can be obtained
at www.ICGtesting.com
Printed in the USA
LVHW070718181119
637667LV00024B/3809/P